Nils-Ole Lund
Collage Architecture

Nils-Ole Lund
Collage Architecture

**with an introduction
by Christian W. Thomsen**

Ernst & Sohn

© 1990 Ernst & Sohn Verlag für Architektur
und technische Wissenschaften, Berlin
ISBN 3-433-02314-X

Type-setting: TypoSatz Bauer GmbH, Fellbach
Colour separation: Hang Ngai Graphic Arts Co., Ltd.,
Hong Kong
Printing and binding: Everbest Printing Co., Ltd.,
Hong Kong

Design: Axel Menges

As a practising architect and later as a critic I have learned how the profession works, where the architects get their ideas and how they translate these ideas into forms. During this process the original content is normally watered down and a gap opens between theory and practice. As architecture is an art of the practicable and the constrained, it cannot of course respond to all new bodies of thought, and when the architects desperately try, their efforts create tensions between content and form, tensions which can be exploited and turned into pictures. In the collages it is possible to mix the world of ideas with the world of building and the resulting imagery can be read in a way which supplements the normal professional dialogue.

The collages I have produced over more than twenty years follow quite closely the changing trends of architectural thinking and practice. They are made out of love to architecture but the love has a touch of irony and distance. As a rather pragmatic Scandinavian I am not friendly towards an architecture which forgets its raison d'être of being an instrument for better environment.

In 1984 Axel Menges from the publishing company Ernst & Sohn saw some of my collages at the exhibition *Bau, Steine, Scherben...* at the Deutsches Architekturmuseum in Frankfurt am Main. He wanted to produce a book on my work right away, but six years passed before it became financially feasible to publish it. A grant from the Danish State Art Foundation and support from Kurt Thorsen A/S made it possible to realize the project.

Professor Christian W. Thomsen from the University of Siegen, who over the years has commented my work with great enthusiasm, has not only undertaken to write the introduction, but shared the task of selecting the collages for the book with Axel Menges.

I would like to thank the sponsors for their generous financial support as well as Christian W. Thomsen and Axel Menges for their continuous efforts in bringing this work to life.

Nils-Ole Lund

Christian W. Thomsen
Nils-Ole Lund: The World as Collage

"Your cities do not exist. Perhaps they have never existed. It is sure they will never exist again. Why do you amuse yourself with consolatory fables?…" (Italo Calvino, *Invisible Cities,* Kublai Khan to Marco Polo)[1]

"For these ports I could not draw a route on the map or set a date for the landing. At times all I need is a brief glimpse, an opening in the midst of an incongruous landscape, a glint of lights in the fog, the dialogue of two passers-by meeting in the crowd, and I think that, setting out from there, I will put together, piece by piece, the perfect city, made of fragments mixed with the rest, of instants separated by intervals, of signals one sends out, not knowing who receives them. If I tell you that the city towards which my journey tends is discontinuous in space and time, now scattered, now more condensed, you must not believe the search for it can stop. …" (Italo Calvino, *Invisible Cities,* Kublai Khan to Marco Polo)[2]

Nils-Ole Lund likes to cook. And he likes to eat and to drink. While placing meat, sauce and rice on the table he remarks: "There is this book by Peter Collins about the analogies of architecture. How architecture is telling stories and how you can form analogies to many theories. The Functionalist theory, for example, and how you can operate with analogies of mechanism, of engines, and so on. And there is his shortest chapter, the analogy between architecture and food. Architects usually don't like it. It doesn't carry enough poetry for them. I like it very much. I think it is the most sensible one. There are fundamental contrasts in food and it is extremely difficult to make a really good dish. You usually start with two contrasting materials and then other ingredients are added." He uncorks a bottle of Bordeaux, puts it on the table, and he continues: "A good meal is a collage. When I start making collages in most cases I have one or two basic pictures, two contrasting images, the rest is added, ideas, details, accessories." His associative way of thinking is jumping forward, sidewards, in spirals: "You get so many nice pictures of food. Post-Modernism, that's an enormous plate of decorated eatables and goodies." And the reader may compare this with his "Ice-Cream Dessert" (621) as a comment on sweet, exchangeable, easily digested and soon forgotten Post-Modern theatrical facades, or the Arcimboldoesque "Academy of Applied Science" (861) where the dinner of living meat and vegetables and fruit and cheese serves as the basis for all those wonderful inventions of a science-oriented consumer-society, or the megaform of his "Gastronomic Landscape" (627) where there are mountains of shrimps and cheese, and hills of garlic, radish parks and a piece of rhubarb thrown into the landscape like Peter Cook's mega-structures from his "Arcadia" projects of the late-seventies, or, to allude to more contemporary design, Daniel Libeskind's Berlin projects which in 1990 have led to the acceptance of his bold Museum of Jewish History. But Lund continues: "New French cooking, that's like reduced and restricted Modernism. For a horrendous price you get very little. They are now rediscovering the regional food of our grandmothers. It's the same in architecture. But I haven't come across Deconstructivist food yet. I wonder what it could look like." He cheers and while we try to arrange the food on our plates in a Deconstructivist manner the conversation floods back to the shores of Lund's distant childhood.

Lund was born in the little town of Ribe near the Danish-German border on 20 August 1930, a date he is very proud of because it was the day of the opening of the first major exhibition which introduced Modernism to Scandinavia, even if little Nils-Ole was not aware of that for some time to come. His father was a historian, his mother a language teacher. The child's reaction consisted in going in for drawing and the building of models, but architecture was by no means a profession he dreamed of as a child. His father was seriously engaged in the anti-German resistance during the years of the German occupation in the Second World War, but even that in Lund's understating remembrance turns into a series of anecdotes and funny incidents.

He studied architecture at the Academy of Fine Arts in Copenhagen from 1948 to 1953. It was the time of the influences of pragmatic Scandinavian Modernists from the thirties like Arne Jacobsen and Gunnar Asplund, and, of course, of Alvar Aalto. As there was little to build in those years, Lund, after serving for two years in the Civil Defense like many of his classmates, went to Norway and Sweden for a period of altogether ten years from 1955 to 1965. In Oslo and Stockholm he participated in the designing of offices and university projects. As a member of Knut Knudsen's team he became familiar with organic nature-oriented Norwegian architecture. In 1962 he visited Japan, and the country's architecture and gardens left a thorough impression on his conceptions of modern architecture.

In 1963 Lund became associate professor in the department of architecture at the Technical University of Trondheim. When in 1965 the school of architecture was founded at Aarhus, Lund was appointed professor at that school and in 1973 was elected vice-chancellor, a position he kept till 1985. In 1965 he also won the first prize in a competition for a new town outside Oslo, a big housing project that kept him busy commuting between Aarhus and Oslo for eight years. Not far from the concept of Bernard Tschumi's La Villette in Paris, Lund calls this project an industrialized system where all the houses though made up for standard modules, could yet be different. And he thinks that in the end that was really too much. Henceforth he stopped designing houses, turned to teaching, writing architectural history, theory, and criticism, and to the making of collages.

The Aarhus school of architecture was originally planned as a small architectural academy for 135 students, yet the 1968 student movement forced the authorities into allowing free entrance for all students and consequently numbers grew to a total of 1000 students, which slowly led to a gradual octopus-like grabbing of neighbourhood buildings which the school mysteriously found its way into. There it spread through rooms and halls never intended for academic and student use, creating a somewhat Kafkaesque, improvised, yet immensely pragmatic and relaxed atmosphere. Over the dozen years when Lund was the school's head he left a decisive mark on its development. Besides this, he is now, in 1990, in his fourth and last year as president of the European Association for Architectural Education.

Lund started making occasional collages in the sixties, but it was a visiting professorship at St. Louis in 1976 which pushed him into producing collages as a result of a culture shock and a means of self-defense in order to survive the more threatening and uncomfortable aspects of the American way of life. While in those years the city of St. Louis was facing racial and industrial crises and, connected with that, a high crime rate, for Lund it looked more and more like a bombed-out community. The students of his traditional architectural school, their system of values still intact, went on designing and drawing beautiful houses. They and their teachers pretended a homogeneity which Lund felt was no longer present in a city where lots of fine old houses had run down and where an annual homicide rate of more than 700 shattered the well-being and the democratic spirit of the citizens. He missed the humane and comparatively undisturbed urbanity of Scandinavian cities like Aarhus. The collage then offered a means to survive with wit and irony, a weapon of satirical criticism which also could be used to draw cultural connections, to intertwine different levels and times in art and architecture.

Artistically the United States of the sixties and early seventies proved very attractive and influential upon Lund. Where Polish painter Wladyslaw Hasior was one of the first to influence his attitude towards the collage in Europe, from the U.S. it was the theory and practice of Pop Art, with Robert Rauschenberg as his favourite exponent, that deeply impressed him. Robert Venturi's book *Complexity and Contradiction in Architecture* (1966) had changed his understanding and his thinking on contemporary architecture in general and on American architecture in particular only a couple of years earlier and was one of the reasons why he went to America at all. Thus his early collage "Venturi Visits Las Vegas" (151) simultaneously represents a homage to Venturi with his dictum "mainstream is almost right" and ambivalent ironical criticism with the image of the truck as a symbol of the forceful virility of macho-erotics, of brutality and American mobility in the centre. The inherent utopian as well as dystopian qualities of his kind of collage offered him a means to discuss historical and contemporary questions and problems of his profession, ethical aspects included. "The collage", Lund says, "can illustrate the distance between the specific utopias of our profession and its actual professional means and possibilities, and, moreover, you can vivisect architectural trends and tendencies by collages whose composed images come closer to actual architecture than the written word."

Through his collages Lund achieved what he could not achieve by teaching – spontaneous feedback reactions of an educated and at least partly informed audience, contacts, discussions in a more direct way than by writing articles, giving lectures or even designing houses. In the years after his stay at St. Louis he became an increasingly professional collage artist and by 1990 he has created more than 900 collages for which he has won critical acclaim in many countries.

By means of his collages he comments on, satirizes, attacks what his profession, architecture, does to landscapes, cities, individual houses. And as that in his opinion is often bad and destructive he has to warn, he has to build up alternative landscapes, cities and houses. Being equipped with more than one identity, Lund creates with the demiurgic voluptuousness of the architect who wants to form the world according to his personal image, and at the same time he attacks, tears down and causes to collapse what he dislikes. He moreover acts with the comprehensive knowledge of an architectural historian and theoretician who makes visible beyond distances in space and time dimensions of artistic and historical depth by putting together seemingly heterogeneous elements into new unities which also develop aesthetic and philosophical qualities of their own. But Lund has yet another soul, that of a clownesque architectural philosopher. Smiling, twinkling, with subtle laughter he implants witty inserts, elements of comic surprise, ironic and absurd ideas into his pictures thereby creating the effect of a quasi-Joycean epiphany. In split seconds they make the viewer aware of hidden contexts and correlations, of tastes put forward by fashions, lobbies, shrewd developers or the Zeitgeist.

According to our general understanding, the principles of collage represent the most central artistic techniques of the twentieth century, in which a plurality of styles and points of view results in a fragmentation of aesthetic and other information and consequently in fragmented consciousness and identity. Fragmentation and the multiplicity of viewpoints on the other hand call for fragmented pictures, the ensemble of which opens new aesthetic dimensions.

Yet Lund combines in his photo-collages seemingly realistic, heterogeneous elements into new homogeneous unities which pretend never to have been heterogeneous. By this method he creates artificial realities, e. g. buildings put together out of fragments of existing buildings, frequently in a strange or exotic environment, which claim to represent buildings that exist. A wonderful example of this is his "Opera-House Below the Sea" (276) where the broken image of Garnier's grand staircase in his Paris opera-house serves as the prototype of an enormous staircase in a festive building, alienated moreover by the grotesque idea of an underwater opera – imagine what happens to voices and instruments – and a fish which swims around and transforms the entire setting into something magically absurd. An alternative to that is the putting of real houses into artificial environments, and natural settings composed of carefully selected fragments to give the effect of an existing natural entity. A good example of the latter is his transformation of "Botta's Circular House" (597) into an imaginary German forest scene. By the way Mario Botta's house is put into nature it achieves, moreover, strange animal-like qualities, looking like some mammal from bygone times left over in a European forest. The story behind that picture is that Botta's house, which was published in architectural magazines all over the globe, has always been photographed in isolation thereby transmitting an incorrect situation to the readers and the architectural public. In reality it stands like an exotic bird in the middle of completely average urban houses, the owners of which feel estranged, inhibited, threatened by the Botta building and have already suggested collecting money to have it torn down. A third alternative consists in collaging fictitious architectural realities, e. g. larger urban constructions, like in the picture with the ironic title "Dreaming of Your Own Home" (194), where the model of Roger Anger's Indian city Auroville as a habitat for the new man of the future (according to the spiritual world image of the Indian philosopher Sri Aurobindo) is combined with fragments of endless suburbias and cityscapes mounted into an ideal landscape.

Lund is convinced that architectural utopias were usually conceived as dreams to improve existing bad housing situations or the socio-economic conditions of urban life. For him utopias regularly turned into nightmares as soon as people tried to realize them. The reason for that lies in the rigidity of uniform concepts which soon reveal intolerant, authoritarian qualities of suppression. Even Scandinavians in their satellite cities are not free from such conceptions, which, of course, in Lund's individualistic opinion are misconceptions. "There are very, very few utopian descriptions which are good", he mutters thoughtfully while preparing the picture for framing.

With paper, a pair of scissors, glue, a thorough knowledge and understanding of art and art history and with a good amount of pictorial wit he experiments in an old-fashioned way with phenomena which nowadays we usually expect to be generated by computer simulation, the creation of photorealistic artificial realities.

He goes even a step further when like in "The Good Habitat 3" (874) he mounts and blends two levels of art and reality, painting and photography, into each other. In the upper part of the picture Le Corbusier's Villa Savoye has a slightly Post-Modern touch by a tower construction which might be an allusion to Mario Botta. The central part consists of a fictitious contemporary interior for the Villa Savoye, a mixture of Bauhaus furniture, fragments of constructional details and spaces which similar to a stage setting generate an atmosphere of authenticity with friendly but irritating Piranesi-like qualities of space, which nevertheless nowhere exist. And into this interior Lund places one of Picasso's woman acts from his Cubist phase in the twenties. The utopian quality of the picture is complicated even more by the Post-Modern side walls of the house and hardly recognizable palm trees. What we are finally offered is a condensed time-space picture-puzzle of art and architectural philosophy that fools the claim of our eyesight to recognize something that could be called reality.

Nevertheless the collage for Lund is a simile for reality, comes pretty close to what reality is in a modern town, in democracy, in a market-oriented liberal economy. A town necessarily has to be a collage, composed of fragments which originally drew their meaning from different contexts. Town planning, the architect and teacher of urban planning in him postulates, can only make sense if it proceeds according to the compositional principles of the collage. You have to construct contrasts, oppositions, transitions, gradually changing developments. If you want to reconstruct a town, you have to accept that collage-like reality and to act in accordance with it when you redevelop urban interconnections.

With a conception like this, city, life and world can only be understood as collages, and here Lund is not far from Italo Calvino's poetic conception of the city as developed in *Invisible Cities* (1972). He proves that the desire for classical harmony may well be a stimulus for a designer, but such classical harmony, at least in a modern context, but perhaps at all times, is mind-conceived, is bogus, does simply not exist. Even in the design of a single house there is the clash of value systems, of different demands for exteriors and interiors. Even the solo house, he realizes, is a collage of counteracting demands and wishes.

In Lund the poetic dreamer, the time-space traveller, the satiric architectural philosopher meets with the artist who has an eye for the grotesque, for the unexpected, for the humorous detail, and with the pictorial storyteller. The result of this complex mix is a multi-talent, which certainly is a narrative but also a highly aesthetic compositeur. Each of his pictures has at least one story behind it, usually it combines several. But they also tell ambivalent stories to the viewer, to whom they offer ample opportunities for differing interpretations. It is fun to trace the origins and allusions, but too much knowledge may even be obstructive to a genuine aesthetic evaluation and enjoyment of his pictures. These collages develop a life of their own and they tell different stories to different people. In some cases even their author has forgotten where the ingredients came from and what they originally meant. At the time he simply selected them for aesthetic reasons or some momentous idea. "Reaching paradise is uninteresting", says down-to-earth, pragmatic realist Lund, "but the road to paradise or to all those other fantastic and exotic places", the artist, dreamer, satirist adds, "may be full of marvellous surprises." And it's those he tries to catch in many of his pictures. In other cases a very carefully constructed composition aims at a particular satirical stroke, usually against fellow architects or architectural fashions and movements.

This may be demonstrated by three of his most beautiful collages, "Flower Arrangement" (745), "Arcadia" (732) and "The Triumph of Post-Modernism" (757).

The first one is a homage to Richard Meier and his High Museum of Art in Atlanta. The museum building is a vase with colourful summer flowers. But the bouquet of flowers, offered to the architect and the public alike, holds a critical moment, too. The building is exquisitely designed and styled, and in the harmony of its proportions, in its playful interior

10

and exterior elegance, in its seeming lightness and airiness it corresponds to the serene grace of the summer flowers. The collage shows Lund's predilection for the charm of classical Modernism in the style of Mies or the early Le Corbusier. But these flowers will soon wither, yet the building, from its inherent demand for timelessness, is not allowed to age. It is not so much the art that is exhibited which counts, as the precious architectonic vessel that puts itself on display, is the message suggested by this collage. And the problem with this kind of virgo-intacta-like Modern architecture is that it necessarily will become deflowered. Air-pollution, wind, weather, the public will stain it with the traces of usage and time. Yet Lund caught it in the prime of early summer, and as it stands it is a love declaration to Richard Meier and the tradition he designs in.

This topic of virginity of pure Modern architecture is also taken up in "Arcadia" where he transplants one of Richard Meier's early masterpieces, the Smith House (1965–67), from its Long Island Sound home into a European pastoral idyll. There is a close correspondence between the girl in the foreground and the rhythmically opened cube of Meier's building, again proclaiming the eternal youth of classical Modernism.

"The Triumph of Post-Modernism" has a stronger satirical grip. Michael Graves' Portland Building as a temple, as a kind of Post-Modern Walhalla, worth the pilgrimage of the community of architecture-worshippers. And at the bottom of the stairs there is the living representation of the figure of "Portlandia" as a naïve version of the "femme fatale". Graves displays in his Portland Building a Post-Modern garden of quotations from Babylon, Egypt, classical Greece, the temples of Aztek cults, Adolf Loos, Art Déco and the Lenin Mausoleum in Moscow. Lund, too, presents it with the claim of the tremendous architectonic success. Born out of the clouds or out of the architectural Big Bang like Venus Anadyomene out of the spray of the Aegean waves. Down there at the stairs we see "Portlandia", who is thought to represent the virtues of Portland in the understanding of the nineteenth century, stretched out with a somewhat silly blush and bloom. Yet this is not Lund's interpretation, who had no idea that Graves designed the figure of the flying "Portlandia" in front of the building's main entrance side. What a coincidence that his blackhaired fashion model, selected for purely aesthetic reasons, because Lund thought her a fit counterpart to Graves' design, looks very much a living version of that sculpture. The interpretation proves that like every work of art Lund's collages are open to different readings according to the foreknowledge and the associative imagination they are confronted with.

The three collages just mentioned are subtle examples of Lund's wit and irony. Even if he attacks he does it with a twinkle in his eyes, with roguish laughter, but never with really scathing sarcasm. His satires are complex, they play with culture, with architecture and art on many levels, they like to set different cultures against each other, so that the viewer may watch, like in a laboratory experiment, what happens when they clash.

Lund's study is dominated by a very large table on which there lie higgledy-piggledy thousands of cuttings and clippings from a wide variety of magazines in a chaotic turmoil. Lund systematically exploits magazines for gentlemen, fashion, art and architecture as well as political journals and advertising brochures. Especially with art magazines he experiences an almost bodily pain when he has to cut them, and he has to pluck up real courage to cannibalize a well designed magazine. That means cutting out even small details, fragments of paintings, interiors, trees, parts of landscapes, sections, parts of buildings, technical installations, fashion, jewellery, women in every situation but preferably naked, and clouds, clouds, clouds. He feels a childlike pride for his collages of clouds.

By a process of filtration and combination these cuttings gradually reach files with captions such as "Monsters", "Naked women" or "Bathing women" or "Flying women", "Caves", "Grottoes", "Waterfalls", "Pop Art", "Post-Modernism", "Classicism". From there, according to his needs, they find their way into collages. Yet this is a working process that involves a lot of hectic puzzles. He starts to look for apt material with a certain idea and the intention of certain effects in his head. Meanwhile he finds an abundance of material for totally different collages other than what he is looking for, while the particular detail he is hunting for may be missing in his collection or he may have it only in a form or variety that does not fit, so that he has to make compromises or to change his plan. Frequently he takes great pains to carefully work out the spirit, the time of design of distinct periods or to kaleidoscope different periods into each other. Talking of classical Modernism, his collage "Functionalism", also called "The International Style" (104), is one of the most brilliant examples.

Other collages are woven into an intricate enigmatic network of symbols and cross references. With yet another group Lund, in the manner of an eighteenth century odd character, takes delight in deceiving onlookers and critics who try to decipher the elements these collages are composed of.

"Functionalism" may serve once more to demonstrate this technique. The viewer who has some knowledge of architectural history may first think that he is looking at Mies van der Rohe, sitting on a Miesian chair in front of the Villa Tugendhat, and he may identify the building in the back as Mies' Villa Wolf. Quite wrong! It is not Mies sitting there, but a British businessman, taken out of a business magazine, the chair is an imitation of a Miesian chair and only a few details of the house originate from Villa Tugendhat. In the background stands an English town-house from the twenties on Californian sand-dunes, but is by no means designed by Mies. A Junkers 52 airplane flies by as a symbol of contemporary High Tech. In Lund's own words "in the twenties they always and everywhere used cars or airplanes." The installation on the lower right hand side of the picture comes from a technical journal and the artist of the collage centre left is not Le Corbusier, as one might presume, but Matisse.

In such a way colleagues and would-be experts are cunningly led astray and made fun of, but simultaneously he creates a condensed, icon-like impression of the late twenties. The monsters, caves, grottoes, and these naked bathing ladies Lund is fond of indeed, they disport themselves for instance as a giant octopus in the piece which is a true example of Lund's delight in the genre of the fantastic with the ironic title "At the Bottom of the Sea" (284). In an Arcadian landscape the sea-monster crushes an architectural land-monstrosity, one of those typical Late-Modern curtain-wall skyscrapers and you imagine to hear the splintering, crashing, crunching noises as the building collapses. Octopusses also symbolize the monstrous growth of highways in the collage "The Traffic System" of 1975.

In "Mysterious Architecture (111) a crocodile is about to bite off that naked beauty's head who is bathing there in a mountain lake in front of a grotto, while in the very next moment an onlooking Nosferatu disappears in the uterine cave above which vaults a karstone landscape, amorphous, ambiguous, as in paintings of Hercules Seeghers. And the ruinous, decadent castle on top of the hill is a mixtum compositum of European and Far-Eastern components. While carefully placing a little crocodile next to another naked lady, Lund comments with a sardonic smile: "I occasionally have to add crocodiles, they are like pepper and spices, they make the picture a little bit hotter."

A southerly, Freudian dreamscape combined of an apocalyptic shimmering polar star, a Neptune's fountain and a Renaissance Bomarzo-like temple-cave entrance is his second piece of "Mysterious Architecture" (504), once more evoking the successful motto of the Gothic novel: "Beauty in the lap of terror." But Lund never read Gothic novels. As a boy he was only fond of the tales of the brothers Grimm and of Rider Haggard's novels, also from the nineteenth century. What he wants to achieve is a strange, fantastic world, a world influenced by the weird conceptions of that famous French postman Ferdinand Cheval and his incredible palace which is a manifestation of all his hidden dreams. Another architectural impression intended is one like in Jean-Jacques Lequeu's bizarre *Architecture civile* (1825), where the most varied architectures are assembled, liberated of their historic, geographic and functional contexts and arranged into a new artificial paper architecture. A further example from his gleeful chamber of horrors, full of Freudian allusions, fragmented architectures, ruins, holes, caves, the stone face of a strange oriental god and a veiled lady doing a somnambulistic dance rounds off his cycle of "Mysterious Architecture" (506). And the monsters of Bomarzo and all those orgies you could imagine in this truly fantastic architectural garden setting, they are never far, they are always subcutaneously alluded to.

Single comments, architectural criticism and satire, the occasional commission for specific purposes, mainly posters for exhibitions or festive events, and series run parallel in Lund's artistic career. Even if a collage looks as unique as "The Green House" (508), where in a most poetic and almost musical way Lund composes and permeates glass architecture, Buckminster Fuller's geodesic domes, organic elements of plants and water, a Classic sculpture and allusions to Classic architecture into each other, such topics and motifs can be found almost everywhere else in his oeuvre.

Among his series two larger ones from the year 1980 are among his most philosophical and most carefully constructed works. It was a time when in academic circles once again concepts of the ideal city were a much discussed topic.

The first series is Lund's answer to the question how he could find the best possible city and how he could develop appropriate town restoration plans. He put a lot of pictorial stories into these collages, as if to support Italo Calvino's view: "The city is redundant: it repeats itself so that something will stick in the mind. … Memory is redundant: it repeats signs so that the city can begin to exist."[3]

He starts this series with a collage called "The Town in the Landscape" (401), which shows a city set into an idyllic mountain scenery, a Russian monastery transforms into Ralph Erskine's Byker Wall looking into Piazza Popolo. Erskine's trade mark, a balloon, hovers above the city.

The second piece, "The Town inside the Walls" (402), presents a particularly harmonious tableau, containing among a few objects difficult to identify parts of the Villa d'Este, of the Alhambra, Erskine's Byker Wall that became so popular in Scandinavian countries, St. Peter, the house of the famous Italian writer D'Annunzio, a figure from a Manet painting. The Italian-style ideal city is changing to "The View from the Wall" (404) and here he took Virginia Woolf's writing place overlooking part of Knole gardens at Vita Sackville-West's palace where she wrote parts of *Orlando.* Despite the emotional turmoil Virginia Woolf reveals in her letters to her lover Vita Sackville-West, the idea of the town in the countryside could hardly look more perfect. One wonders whether our collage artist had read Virginia Woolf's letters. In one of them she writes:

"Dearest Honey,

Why do you write a letter on Wednesday and I only get it on Monday?…

It's this damned *Orlando* – I want to finish it, and I can't finish it; and then I wake in the night so excited and have to take a sleeping draught and so spend my day moping. But we are going to Rodmell for three or four days and there – please God – you'll be finished off; and I shall come back refreshed. I rather think, too, it's an addled egg: too hasty, too splash-dashery, and all over the place. But I shall put it in a drawer till May. Why lecture the Danes on poetry when you might give Virginia (who is worth all Copenhagen) a practical demonstration in the art of love?…"[4]

What this demonstrates is how one can spin off narratives from these pictures which are not necessary for their understanding but add to the artistic flavour.

The fourth collage represented here is called "The Ruins of the Town" (405) and Lund collected all kinds of ruins from Rome and elsewhere to synthesize them in this picture together with accessories like waterfalls, the beautiful lady-sculpture with her many children from Copenhagen's Glyptothek, a group of tourists and Lund's beloved crocodile.

Next in this series comes a collage entitled "The Boulevard" (406). It looks like a complete entity but it is composed of houses from America and Venice, a Berlin painting by Max Liebermann and an English tea-drinking advertising. As far as the overall concept of the ideal city is concerned this collage makes it evident that such a concept has nothing to do with a town being new. On the contrary, urbanity, it is suggested, contains its inbuilt ageing processes.

"The Big Sun Collector" (407) ist the sixth collage of this series, which contains his version of a future-oriented technology mounted on famous La Coruña houses and is Lund's ironic contribution to the green movement. Isadora Duncan dances on a spring meadow filled with flowers, her well-known scarf fluttering in the breeze. It was eventually to cost her her life when she was driving in her Alfa Romeo convertible and it became entangled in a tree and strangled her to death. The ideal city, is the message here, has to find new, soft energy technologies in order to survive.

And finally there is the collage with the title "The Space of the Town" (409) which like a Piranesi grown friendly contains lots of city spaces taken from the Dutch architect Hertzberger as well as from the Ford Foundation and a number of other places. It points out how essential the interplay of indoor–outdoor spaces is for man's comfort and well-being.

The idea behind the entire series is that anti-utopian concept of an ideal city not consisting of pre-planned, uniform elements – think what would have become of Paris if Le Corbusier's ideas had been realized – but of an ingenious laissez-faire time-space collage. The second series, called "Collage City" (414, 415, 420 – 423), may look self-explanatory, but Lund put a lot of philosophical thinking into it concerning "mapping" and how to connect pieces in a collage as well as in a city. He was certainly influenced by Colin Rowe's book *Collage City,* but also puts forward plenty of his own ideas. All of these cityscapes are poetic, yet the most poetic of them all, a very Turneresque piece, again recalls memories of Calvino: "…and in his dreams now cities light as kites appear, pierced cities like laces, cities transparent as mosquito netting, cities like leaves' veins, cities lined like a hand's palm, filigree cities to be seen through their opaque and fictitious thickness."[5]

Contrary to Bernard Tschumi who thinks architecture the only erotic medium left at all, connecting architecture, beautiful women and fashion is as much a predilection of Lund – right from his beginnings up to the present day – as using that set of motifs associated with food. Whether they wear mundane or slightly crazy architectural hats (307, 312, 545) or display the detached beauty of their own architectural build (473) in front of cool Modernism, whether they stay "Clean and Cool" (172) with germfree, sterile Modernist high-rises or voluptuously spread their legs, heavily perfumed in front of Charles Moore's Post-Modern monument Piazza d'Italia (480), or whether they act as an "Architectural Call-Girl" (824), the symbol of decadent Modernism turned into architectural prostitution, Lund criticizes, satirizes that kind of architecture which goes for the easy solution. Simultaneously he is attracted by fashion and its ambivalence as soon as it shows "class". From that point of view the Chicago high-rise beauty queen wearing gold all over is as attractive as Helmut Jahn and Philip Johnson whose models are constantly changing dresses.

Philip Johnson's unscrupulous agility and adaptability to all current mainstreams which lead him from Functionalist Bauhaus coolness to the sultry pleasure gardens of Post-Modernism and thence to the risky equilibria of Deconstructivism is satirized with ingenious elegance in Lund's collage "The Fashion of Architecture" (781). One of Johnson's latest high-rises, the so-called "lipstick-building" at the corner of 53rd Street and Third Avenue in Manhattan, where meanwhile the office of the firm Johnson/Burgee Architects is located, appears in this collage as a long skirt of winter fashion – Johnson himself is not the youngest of his profession – worn by a beautiful, but extremely arrogant looking model, who otherwise is dressed in an expensive, dark brown Persian lambskin coat. It may be an overinterpretation, but who so wishes may even recognize a political allusion in that, to Johnson's affiliation with fascism in the thirties. Many critics still accuse him of proto-fascist thinking. But the elegance of the master who calls architecture "an old man's game" is undeniable.

Another thematically quite different series of eight collages from 1987 is the one called "Elegies". What Lund describes here is the transmutation of female bodies into landscapes, rocks, trees, waterfalls, and architectures interwoven with ageing processes. Exquisitely tasteful, this is bound into an atmosphere of melancholy sadness. Human bodies, like architectures, inevitably grow old, yet if this happens with dignity, they keep a specific beauty at every stage of this transformation process.

Ruins always had a fascination for Lund. Like the eighteenth-century garden architect he feels attracted by the mysterious qualities of collapsing, worn-out, withering buildings. And it is not just classical ruins he appreciates as in his series "Mysterious Architecture". In monuments of Modernism he often satirizes, as just mentioned above, the fact that they cannot age with grace and dignity, that they do not even produce beautiful ruins like Classicism. When he demonstrated this in the small series "The Future of Architecture" of 1980, bought by the Deutsches Architekturmuseum in Frankfurt, with Louis Kahn's "Salk Institute", with James Stirling's "Leicester Engineering Building" and the anonymous "Skyscraper on the Rocks" (282), he for a while became a favourite artist of Heinrich Klotz, who in the mid-eighties acted as the German protagonist of Post-Modernism. Klotz mistook Lund's basic interest in the ambiguity of ruins for an attack on Modernism. Lund's position, however, was one that pointed out the irresistibility of age and destruction. His reproach was directed against the shabbiness of ageing Modern buildings, but it was not a plea for Post-Modernism. When this became evident, Klotz lost his interest in Lund.

After all that has been said it would look strange if a character like Lund did not make fun of his fellow-architects, too. And, of course, he does. Danish culture has always been influenced by surrounding countries, mainly by its Scandinavian neighbours and by Britain and Germany. Coming from rural, agrarian and seafaring roots, despite all these pressures, it has never lost its specific identity and in the twentieth century this small country has produced an amazing line of outstanding architects. To mention but a few of the internationally best known we should point out Arne Jacobson, Jørn Utzon, C.F. Møller, Jørgen Bo, Wilhelm Wohlert, Hans Dissing, Otto Weitling and Henning Larsen. Whereas the design of Danish housing follows rather traditional lines, public buildings, industrial buildings, cultural buildings follow international trends.

"The Architect Johan Richter" (749), sitting surrounded by his models with a glass of whisky-soda – a lot of soda, a little whisky – is only a mild joke, "The Architect Knud Friis" (768), standing in front of the Berlin Wall together with some of his bunkerlike Brutalism, comes out as a much stronger statement, whereas "The Architect C.F. Møller" (867) appears as a real monument, but it is only his head and hardly the Aarhus church it is sitting on that is so monumental. "The Architect Niels Torp" (823), with his three Graces, mirrors Lund's collages "Four Times Classicism" (747, 809), turning Classicist buildings into a somewhat mediocre variety of Post-Modernism. The best of these insider jokes, however, is one called "Five Norwegian Architects Waiting for the Archetype" (587). Norwegians and archetypes obviously belong together. And there they sit in the middle of a forest around a table with the model of a rather unimaginative Modernist building before them. And finally the archetype appears, a huge ugly toad or bullfrog. A palette of ambiguous feelings is mirrored in their faces from scepticism and amazement to sheer happiness. As a joke this is one of Lund's best. Into this category also belongs the collage "An English Gentleman Architect Is Returning to the Dry Shores of Classicism" (590). With a kind of prophetic foresight Lund here seems to have forecasted the revival of British Classicism and that fervent debate about Prince Charles' conception according to which Classicism should be the eternal form of British architecture and the architectural balm for the High-Tech-ridden souls of city dwellers and country folks alike.

The treatment of Louis Kahn (628), James Stirling (630) and Mies van der Rohe (632) is a different one. These master builders are depicted as such, yet dealt with in a mixture of deep reverence and ambiguous irony. The detail is just hilarious: Louis Kahn and his lion in a forest scenery, James Stirling looking up to God the Almighty, asking for advice and standing next to a waterfall. The building surrounding him is the Cambridge University Library, visually attractive, but suffering from leakages to such a degree that time and again the authorities responsible considered having it torn down. And Mies the Great sits in deep contemplation in front of a torrential waterfall and one of his early high-rise designs, next to him his free-swinging chair as a model of timeless elegance and functionalism. He clearly waits for some final inspiration.

The debate between Modernism and Post-Modernism is constantly reflected in Lund's collages of the eighties. What is curiously lacking is his comment on High Tech and Deconstructivism. There is one treatment of Foster's Hong Kong and Shanghai Bank called "Heavy Metal" (812), emerging out of Max Ernst's primeval jungle while a vulture-like bat is crying havoc on top of a rocky mountain. It is a very dramatic picture in which Foster's building looks like a threatening metal sculpture, but hardly a discussion or satirical analysis of High Tech.

Among Lund's late collages so far there are two enigmatic and poetic pieces (894, 895) referring to Stephen Spender's poem *The Pylons* (1933) where in a mood of deep cultural

Notes

[1] Italo Calvino, *Invisible Cities*, translated from the Italian by William Weaver, London, 1979, p. 48.
[2] Ibid., p. 126.
[3] Ibid., p. 1 f.
[4] Nigel Nicolson (ed.), *A Change of Perspective. The letters of Virginia Woolf,* volume III: 1923–1928, London, 1977, p. 468.
[5] Italo Calvino, op. cit., p. 58.
[6] "The Pylons" in: *Stephen Spender. Collected Poems 1928–1985,* London and Boston, 1985, p. 39.

scepticism he has a presentiment of something like the dawn of a post-industrial cityscape:

"Dreaming of cities
Where clouds shall lean their swan-like neck". [6]

What does this mean? Is he tired of playing the satirist? Or are his swans in fact attacking gilded prototypes of functional Modernism? Lund turns round smiling and in one of his associative jumps he remarks: "It's not a good time to write on deserts". "Why?" "Openness, you know, complete openness…" And he chuckles with his throaty laughter like a Norwegian troll.

"All the world's a stage", Shakespeare said (*As You Like It,* II. Vii, 139).

Lund not only manages to put an icon of Art Déco architecture like the Chrysler building on a beautiful lady's head (311), so that the two beauties look the perfect integration of stylized human and architectural build, he also endows a traditional topic like "The Tower of Babel" of 1974 with a new philosophical meaning. His "babelstårn" is neither an incomplete fragment nor a ruin. It has been completed, it is a place to live in, a synthesis of orient and occident, a place where old and new, buildings sacred and secular, pagodas and extravaganzas meet. To cut a long story short: His Tower of Babel is "Collage City". And finally he takes modern satellite telecommunication, buildings and cities from different cultures and times plus a globe (814) and he arrives at a new twist of Shakespeare's well-known simile: "All the world's a collage."

The Tower of Babel. After 1970. 95 x 59 cm
The Traffic System. 1975. 60 x 59 cm

104. Functionalism. After 1975. 50 x 64 cm
107. Art Nouveau. 1978. 50 x 70 cm

166. A Nude in a Decorated Setting.
1976. 44 x 58 cm
172. Clean and Cool. 1976. 33 x 29 cm

174. A Young Couple is Rowing Away from the
Grounded Boston City-Hall. 1976. 40 x 53 cm
194. Dreaming of Your Own Home. 1977. 50 x 70 cm

196. Paradisiac Architecture. 1977. 67 x 34 cm
276. Opera-House Below the Sea. 1979. 45 x 37 cm

pp. 30, 31
282. Skyscraper on the Rocks. 1979. 50 x 37 cm
284. At the Bottom of the Sea. 1979. 48 x 34 cm

32

297. The Invention of the Bulb. 1979. 60 x 42 cm
307. An Architectural Hat. 1979. 58 x 24 cm

311. An Architectural Hat. 1979. 50 x 21 cm
312. An Architectural Hat. 1979. 43 x 35 cm

401. The Town in the Landscape. 1980. 49 x 69 cm

404. The View from the Wall. 1980. 49 x 69 cm

406. The Boulevard. 1980. 49 x 69 cm

409. The Space of the Town. 1980. 49 x 69 cm
414. Collage City. 1980. 35 x 51 cm

43

415. Collage City. 1980. 35 x 51 cm

420. Collage City. 1980. 35 x 51 cm

422. Collage City. 1980. 35 x 51 cm

50

473. A Beauty and a New-Corbusier House. 1982.
32 x 33 cm

480. The Beauty and Post-Modernism. 1982.
63 x 45 cm

488. First the Building and Then the Site. 1982.
51 x 25 cm
496. A Monument in Search of a Meaning. 1982.
41 x 35 cm

504. Mysterious Architecture. 1982
506. Mysterious Architecture. 1982. 52 x 37 cm

508. The Green House. 1982. 57 x 37 cm
549. The Aarhus Opera-House as Ruin. 1982.
39 x 50 cm

587. Five Norwegian Architects Waiting for the
Archetype. 1983. 44 x 62 cm
590. An English Gentleman Architect Is Returning
to the Dry Shores of Classicism. 1983. 41 x 53 cm

NOL 597 JULI 1983

607. Fundamentalism. 1983. 51 x 66 cm

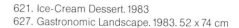

pp. 68, 69
628. In Honour of Louis Kahn. 1983. 51 x 37 cm
630. In Honour of James Stirling. 1983. 51 x 37 cm

632. In Honour of Mies van der Rohe. 1983.
51 x 37 cm
637. The Staircase. 1984. 35 x 50 cm

pp.72,73
655. A Course of Architecture. 1984. 66 x 32 cm
698. The Danish House. 1984. 52 x 38 cm

732. Arcadia. 1985. 35 x 50 cm
742. The Mouth in the Mountain. 1985. 94 x 67 cm

pp. 80, 81
749. The Architect Johan Richter. 1985. 100 x 69 cm.
(Photo of the architect: Poul Pedersen)
757. The Triumph of Post-Modernism. 1985.
69 x 51 cm

760. The Road of Architecture. 1985. 96 x 48 cm
763. The Mountain. 1986. 99 x 69 cm

768. The Architect Knud Friis. 1986. 121 x 73 cm.
(Photo of the architect: Poul Pedersen)
779. The Fashion of Architecture. 1986

pp. 86, 87
780. The Fashion of Architecture. 1986. 36 x 26 cm
781. The Fashion of Architecture. 1986. 36 x 26 cm

NOL maj 86 T81.

Noh maj '86 780

783. A Course of Post-Modern Architecture. 1986.
58 x 59 cm

788. Trouble in Heaven. 1986. 70 x 33 cm

805. Elegy 3. 1987. 89 x 66 cm
806. Architectural Outlook. 1987. 40 x 43 cm

pp. 94, 95
808. Danish Building Research Institute. 1987. 79 x 56 cm
809. Four Times Classicism. 1987. 79 x 71 cm

pp. 96, 97
812. Heavy Metal. 1987. 70 x 50 cm
814. The Office-Building of the Future. 1987. 69 x 49 cm

pp. 98, 99
816. Elegy 4. 1987. 69 x 49 cm
817. Elegy 5. 1987. 69 x 49 cm

823. The Architect Niels Torp. 1987. 79 x 69 cm
824. Architectural Call-Girl. 1987. 42 x 43 cm

867. The Architect C. F. Møller. 1988. 69 x 100 cm.
(Photo of the architect: Poul Pedersen)
872. The Good Habitat 1. 1989. 35 x 50 cm

873. The Good Habitat 2. 1989. 35 x 50 cm

887. The Housing "Garvergården". 1989. 50 x 37 cm
893. Henning Larsen and Chirico. 1990. 33 x 45 cm

pp. 110, 111
894. Dreaming of Cities Where Often Clouds
Shall Lean Their Swan-Like Neck. 1990. 58 x 47 cm
895. Dreaming of Cities Where Often Clouds
Shall Lean Their Swan-Like Neck. 1990. 49 x 43 cm